This book belong to

Este libro pertenece a:

____

Pollito—Chick

By: Maria Aduke Alabi

To order additional copies of this book, visit www.QuisqueyanaPress.com/Tienda or contact:

Quisqueyana Press
Poway, California 92064
info@quisqueyanapress.com
www.quisqueyanapress.com

ISBN 978-1-7354562-4-9

2nd. edition

Library of Congress Control Number: 2020909608

(Aprende Ingles cantando)

Pollito

Chick

(Learn Spanish Singing)

MARIA ADUKE ALABI

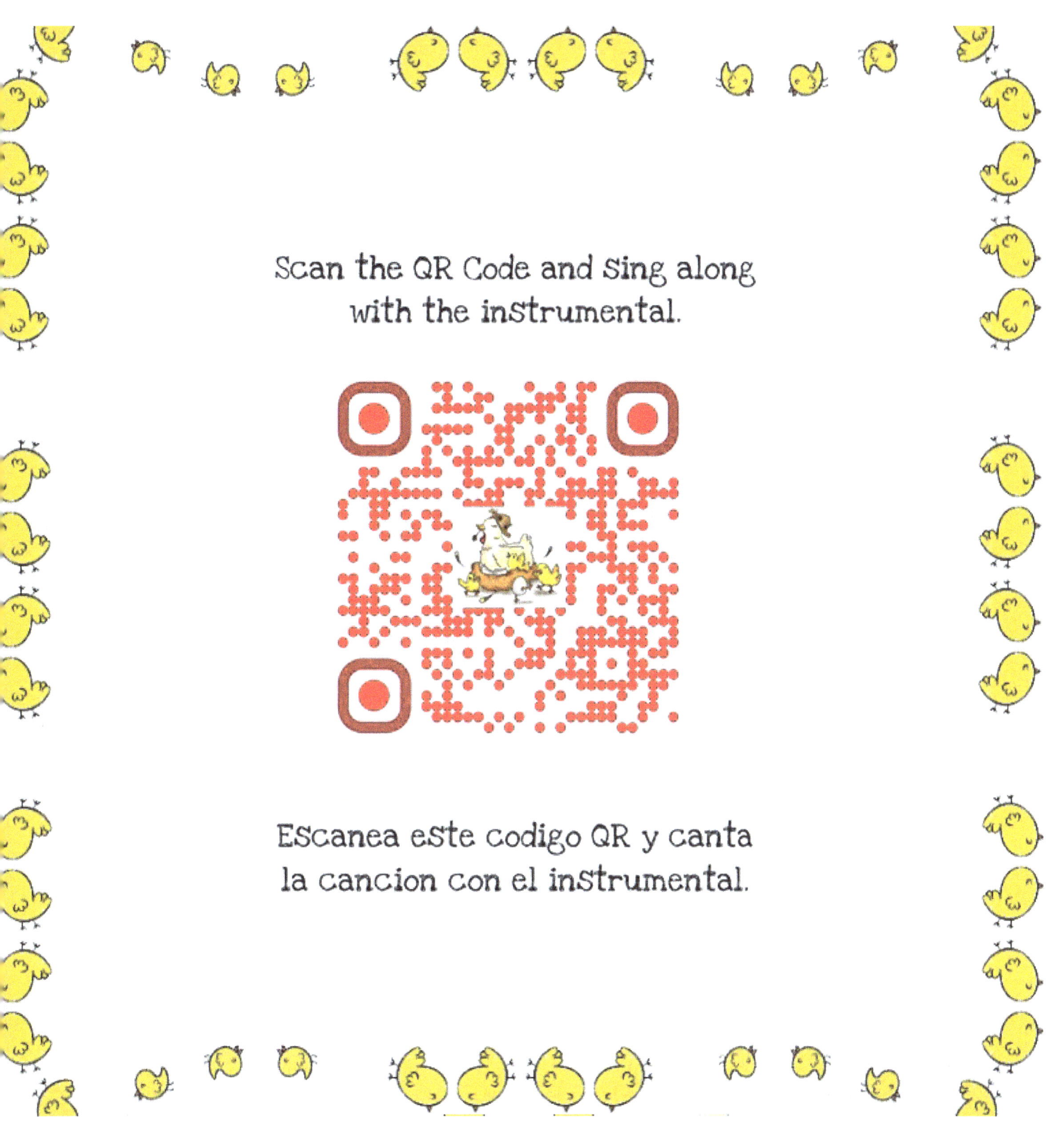

Scan the QR Code and Sing along
with the instrumental.

Escanea este codigo QR y canta
la cancion con el instrumental.

Pollito— Chick
(Pojito)

Gallina— Hen

(Gajena)

Lápiz— Pencil

(Lapith)

Y Pluma— Pen

(e)

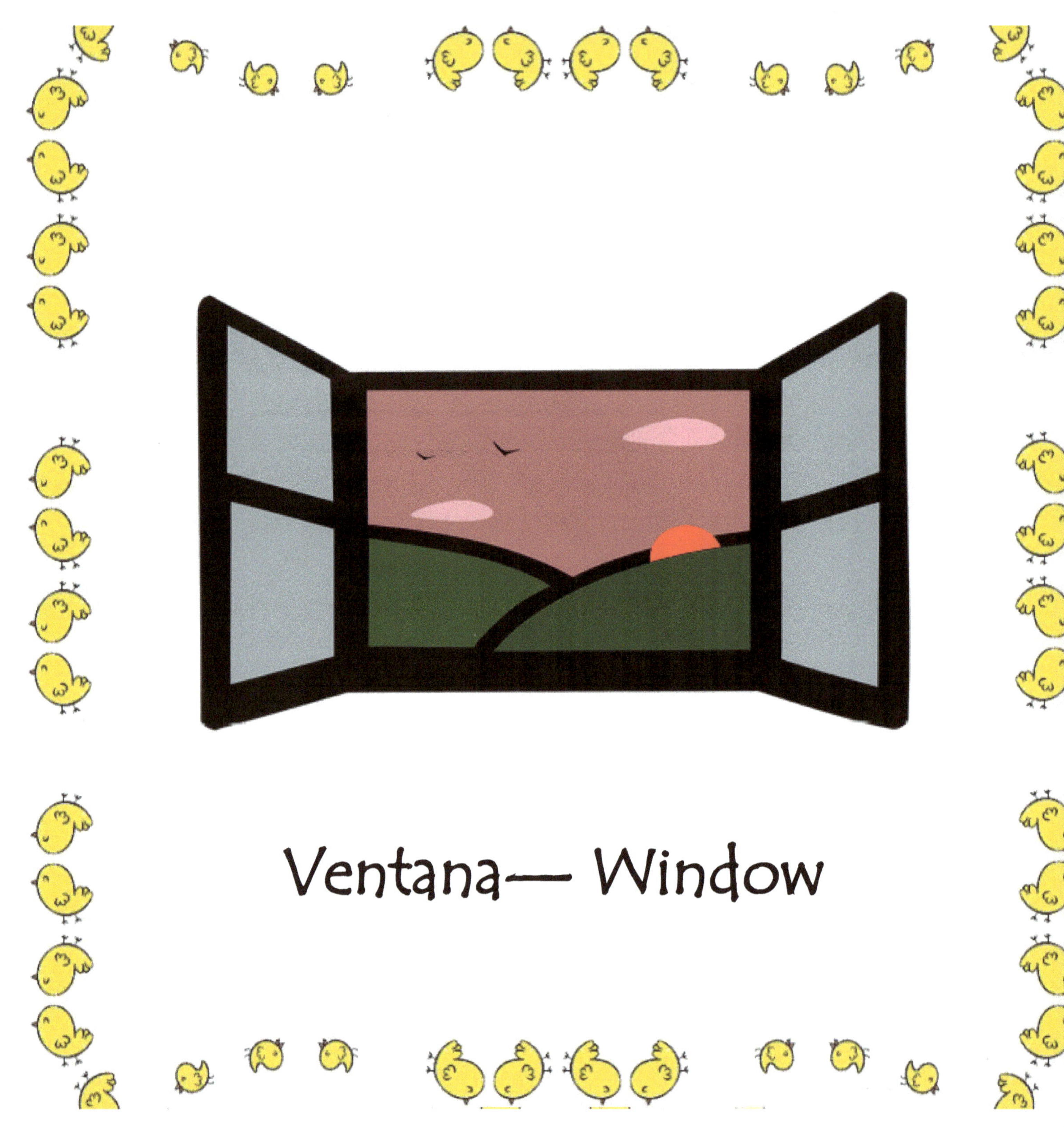

Ventana— Window

Puerta— Door

Techo
ceiling
(siiling)
Y (e)
Piso
floor

Almohada— Pillow

(pilou)

Cama— Bed

Mesa— Table

(Teibol)

Y Silla— Chair

(e) (sija)   (Chear)

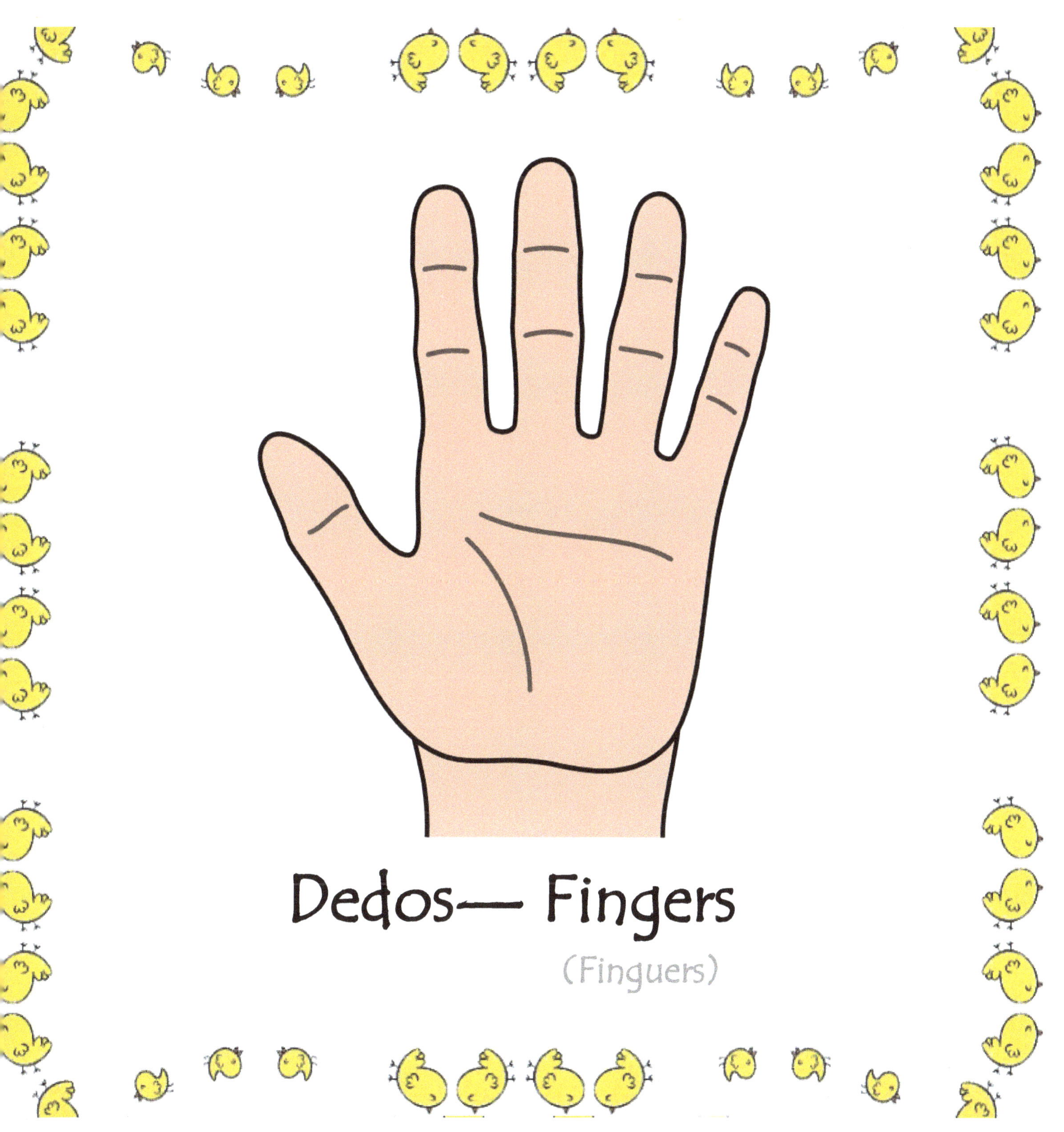

Dedos— Fingers

(Finguers)

Cabeza— Head

(Hed)

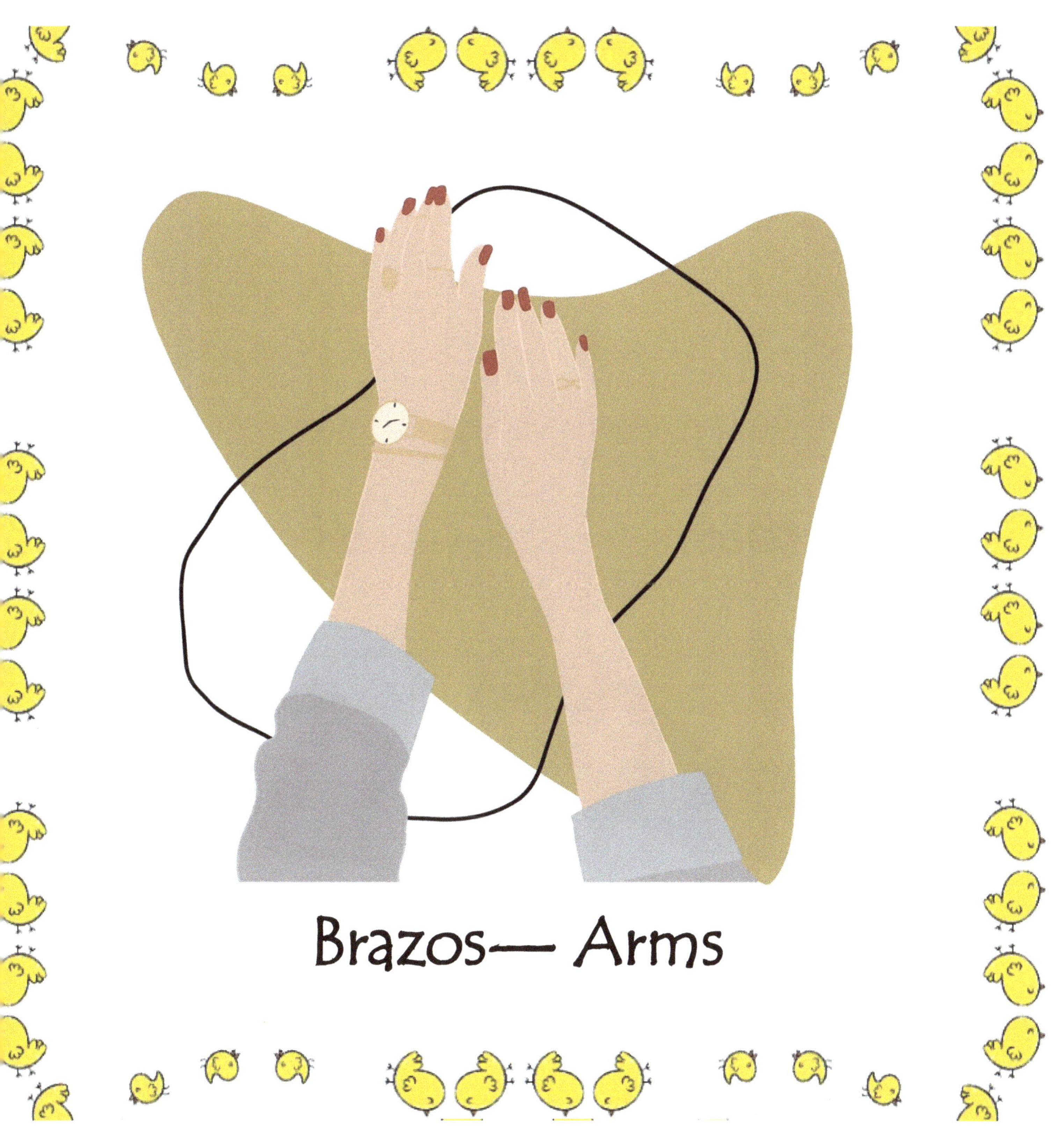

Brazos— Arms

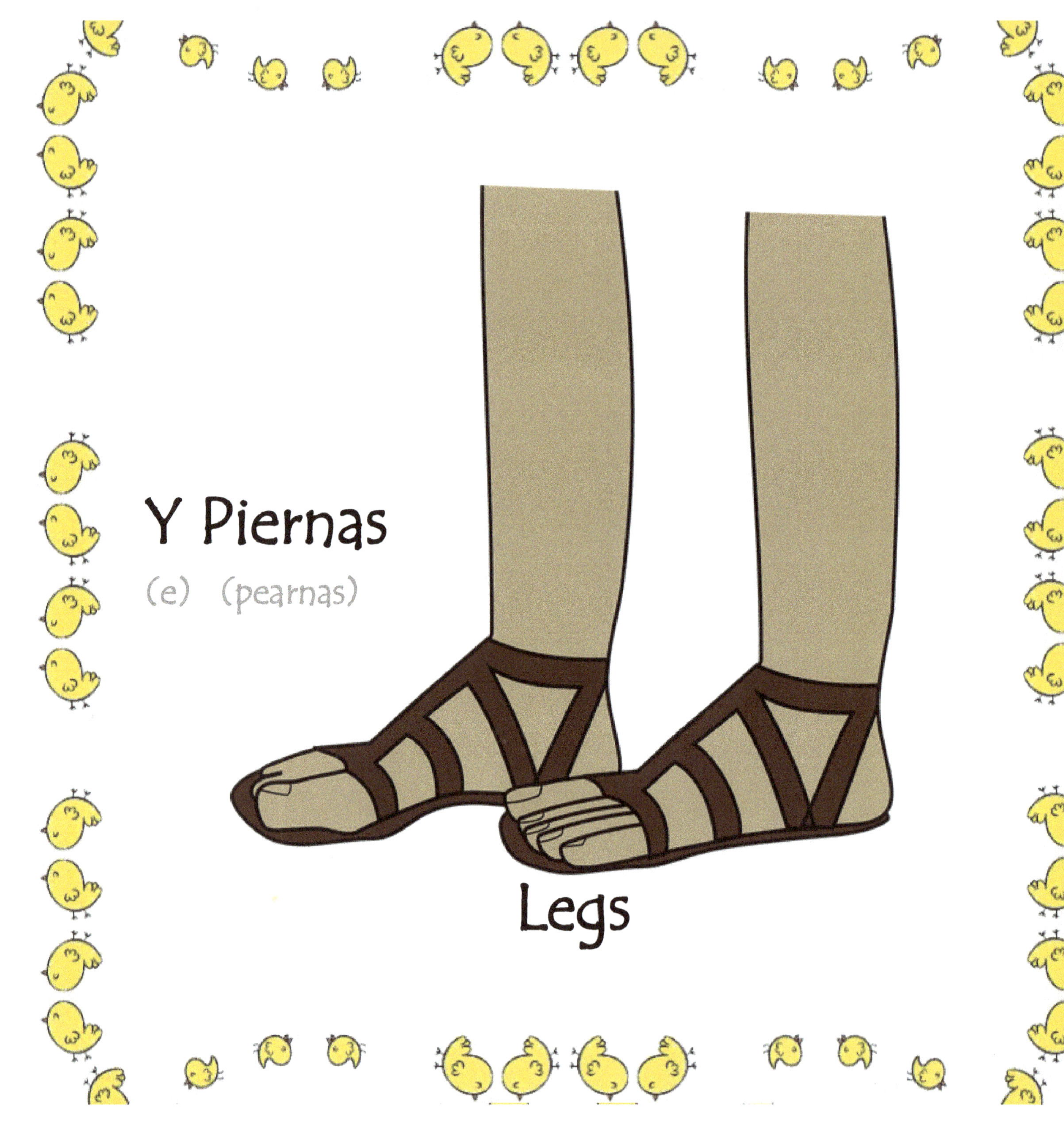
Y Piernas
(e) (pearnas)
Legs

Caldero— Pot

(calthero)

Rana— Frog

Pato— Duck

(Dok)

Y Muñeca— Doll

(e)

Vocales— Vowels

(vawols)

Mosca— Fly

(Flai)

Sol— Sun

(son)

Y Tiempo— Time

(e) (Taim)

Aquí termina
Here is the end
(Hear is de end)

Adios amigos
Goodbye my friends
(Gudbay mai frends)

POLLITO CHICKEN
Canción Infantil Tradicional
Lucía Gomes
Piano
Po - lli - to chi - cken Ga - lli - na hen La - piz pen - cil
y plu - ma pen. Ven - ta - na win - dow Puer - ta door
te - cho cei - ling y pi - so floor Al - mo ha - da pi - llow
Ca - ma bed Me - sa ta - ble y si - lla chair
De - dos fin - gers Ca - be - za head Bra - zos arms
y pier - nas legs. Ha si - do to - do this is the end.
a - qui ter - mi - na good - bye my friend
www.quisqueyanapress.com

The Song - La Cancion
Español & English

Pollitos - Chicks
Gallina - Hen
Lapiz - Pencil
y Pluma - Pen

Ventana - Window
Puerta - Door
Techo - Ceiling
y Piso - Floor

Almohadas - Pillows
Cama - Bed
Mesa - Table
y Silla - Chair

Dedos - Fingers
Cabeza - Head
Brasos - Arms
y Piernas - Legs

Caldero - Pot
Rana - Frog
Pato - Duck
y Muñeca - Doll

Vocales - Vowels
Mosca - Fly
Sol - Sun
y Tiempo - Time

Aqui Termina - This is the end
Adios Amigos - Goodbye my friends

Image attributions:
Celing and Floor:
<a href="https://www.vecteezy.com/free-vector/kid">Kid
Vectors by Vecteezy</a>

Pillow: <a
href="https://www.vecteezy.com/free-vector/pillow">Pillow
Vectors by Vecteezy</a>

Colección:

"Melodías Infantiles Tradicionales"

Para aprender cantando.

Otros libros de la colección:

"Uno, Dos, Tres Amigos— One, Two, Three Friends"